WARTIME SPIES

CREATIVE EDUCATION • CREATIVE PAPERBACKS

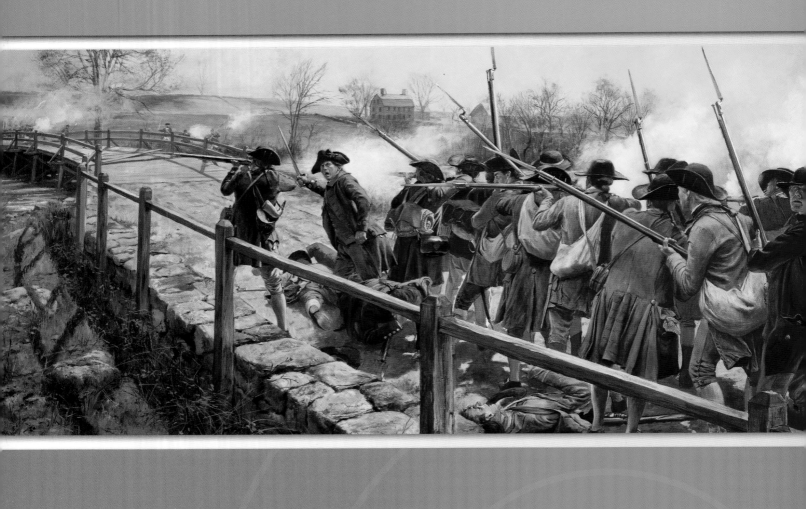

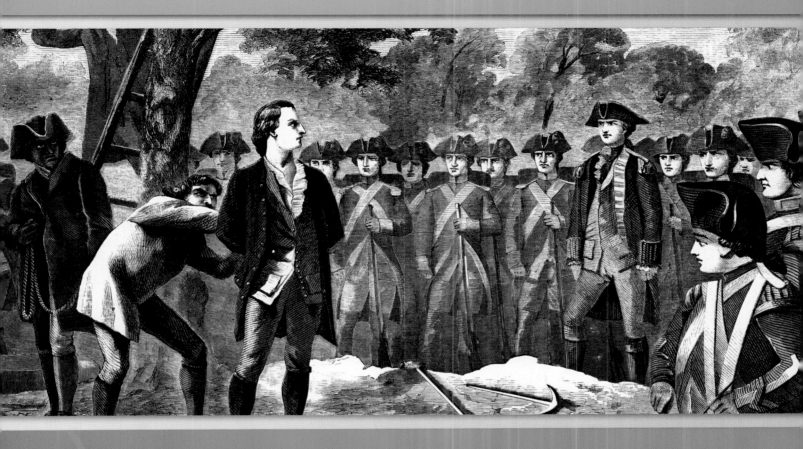

REVOLUTIONARY WAR SPIES

MICHAEL E. GOODMAN

Published by Creative Education and Creative Paperbacks
P.O. Box 227, Mankato, Minnesota 56002
Creative Education and Creative Paperbacks are imprints of
The Creative Company
www.thecreativecompany.us

Design and production by Chelsey Luther
Art direction by Rita Marshall
Printed in Malaysia

Photographs by Alamy (North Wind Picture Archives), Bridgeman
Art Library (Christie's Images), Corbis (Bettmann, Corbis, Graphi-
caArtis, National Geographic Society, Tarker, Don Troiani), Dream-
stime (Ironjohn), Getty Images (Louis S. Glanzman, Hulton Archive,
Lambert, Time & Life Pictures, UniversalImagesGroup), Library of
Congress (Newcastle, Prints & Photographs Division, The Universal
Magazine of Knowledge and Pleasure), Lost & Taken (Brant Wilson),
Shutterstock (Georgios Kollidas), SuperStock (Universal Images
Group), TextureX.com (TextureX), VectorTemplates.com, Wikime-
dia Creative Commons (John Foxe)

Library of Congress Cataloging-in-Publication Data
Goodman, Michael E.
Revolutionary War spies / Michael E. Goodman.
p. cm. — (Wartime spies)
Summary: A historical account of espionage during the Revolu-
tionary War, including famous spies such as Nathan Hale, covert
missions, and technologies that influenced the course of the conflict.
Includes bibliographical references and index.
ISBN 978-1-60818-601-3 (hardcover)
ISBN 978-1-62832-206-4 (pbk)
1. United States—History—Revolution, 1775-1783—Secret service—
Juvenile literature. 2. Spies—United States—History—18th centu-
ry—Juvenile literature. I. Title.

E279.G66 2014
973.3'85—dc23   2014037534

CCSS: RI.5.1, 2, 3, 5, 6, 8; RH.6-8.3, 4, 5, 6, 7, 8, 9

First Edition HC 9 8 7 6 5 4 3 2 1
First Edition PBK 9 8 7 6 5 4 3 2 1

CONTENTS

DODGING DANGER

On a dark night in October 1776, an American patrol surrounded a house where a band of *Tories* was meeting. The patrol had been alerted to the meeting by *Patriot* spy Enoch Crosby, who was working undercover inside the Tory group. In spy terms, that made him a *mole*. During the raid, Crosby was discovered hiding in a closet and was marched out in chains. Just before being imprisoned, he showed his captors a pass signed by John Jay, the leader of American *counterespionage*. Crosby passed along his secrets; then he was returned to custody and told to escape on his own. Hours later, Crosby forced open a window and slid silently to the ground below. He had gone only 50 yards (45.7 m) when an American sentry shouted, "Halt!" and opened fire. Crosby dodged the bullets and desperately raced to safety. The next day, he was back to being a colonial shoemaker supposedly loyal to the British king.

TERRIBLE TAXES BUILD BAD FEELINGS

THE FIRST SHOTS OF the Revolutionary War were exchanged on April 19, 1775, between British soldiers and Patriot *Minutemen* during the Battles of Lexington and Concord in Massachusetts. But the war had been building for 12 years. In February 1763, British, French, and Spanish leaders signed the Treaty of Paris, ending the French and Indian War (1756–63). The war had been costly, and Great Britain felt that the American colonies should help pay off the debt incurred while fighting on their soil. King George III urged Britain's Parliament to impose taxes on the colonists, who had no representation in the government. One new law, the Stamp Act of 1765, levied a tax on printed materials such as newspapers, calendars, marriage licenses, pamphlets, and playing cards.

So named for their immediate reaction to threats, the Minutemen set out for battle straight from home.

Angry Americans formed secret Sons of Liberty clubs throughout the colonies to oppose the Stamp Act. Several colonial leaders were printers and newspaper publishers who showed their opposition by printing *propaganda* that ridiculed Great Britain and fired up Americans. Soon, women's groups called Daughters of Liberty were formed. Their members vowed not to marry any man who bought products made in Great Britain. The British quickly rescinded the law in 1766, but other hated tax laws followed. In opposition to a tax placed on tea in 1773, Sons of Liberty members disguised as American Indians boarded British ships and threw 340 chests of expensive English tea into Boston Harbor.

From that point on, hostilities escalated. British troops crossed the Atlantic to take control in Boston, and colonial leaders met in Philadelphia to discuss a unified response to Britain's actions. Committees of Safety were formed throughout the colonies to organize *militias*, and Patriot spies helped locate and steal British weapons and supplies. On June 15, 1775, George Washington was named commander in chief of American troops. Two days later, a bloody battle at Bunker Hill in Boston marked the start of real fighting.

COVERT OPS
CODING BY THE BOOK

Benedict Arnold coded his messages to his British contact, Major John André. Each coded word in a message would be represented by three numbers separated by periods. To *decipher* the code, André used the book *Blackstone's Commentaries on the Laws of England*. The numbers referred to a page number, line number, and word number on that line in the book. For example, 288.9.9 meant page 288, line 9, word 9 and stood for "west." Here is one coded sentence from an Arnold letter and its hidden meaning: "I 149.8.7 10.8.22'd the 57.9.71 at 288.9.9, 198.9.26." (*I have accepted the command at West Point.*)

CHAPTER ONE
A PERFECT ENVIRONMENT *for* ESPIONAGE

WHEN THE REVOLUTIONARY WAR began, the odds for an American victory were pretty slim. The British army was manned by professional soldiers from Great Britain ("Redcoats") and *mercenaries* brought in mostly from the German state of Hesse ("Hessians"). The American army consisted primarily of colonial farmers, laborers, and craftsmen drafted into service. The Americans had fewer soldiers, fewer experienced military leaders, fewer weapons, and less money to finance the war. So how did they win? Major George Beckwith, Britain's top spy in America during the Revolution, explained it this way: "George Washington did not really outfight the British; he simply outspied us!"

The war fought in the American colonies was a perfect environment for espionage. First of all, almost as many colonists opposed the Revolution as supported it. John Adams, a Boston lawyer and future United States president, estimated that about one-third of the colonists favored independence, one-third wanted to stay connected to Great Britain, and one-third were neutral. So it was often easy to recruit someone with strong views to spy against the opposition. Secondly, most colonists—whether Patriot or Tory—spoke the

Revolutionary War soldiers were willing to follow George Washington's every lead.

same language, wore similar clothes, and shared the same heritage. This made it easy for a spy on either side to blend in with the enemy.

Both the Americans and the British were spying on each other before the war even began, and espionage helped lead to the fighting in Lexington and Concord. Several weeks before the battles, a British spy had informed General Thomas Gage, the royal governor of Massachusetts, that the Americans were storing weapons and ammunition in Concord. The American spy network in Boston, led by silversmith Paul Revere, learned that Gage planned to make a raid on Concord. The local militiamen were put on the alert and were ready to fight back when the British arrived at Concord Bridge on the morning of April 19, 1775.

Throughout the war, both sides relied on spies to gather information and to trick the other side with disinformation— false or misleading *intelligence*. Both sides also reserved money to organize *spy rings* and pay individual spies. For example, one of the first budget requests that George Washington made after being named commander in chief was for $333 1/3 to pay for spies to operate in Boston. (That would be around $10,700 in today's money.) Washington always paid his spies well and paid them promptly. That helped keep them loyal and ensured they would

not become *double agents*.

Washington put the spying budget to work right away when he discovered in September 1775 that the American army had only 36 barrels of gunpowder on hand to withstand a potential British attack on Boston. He hired civilian spies to mingle among Tories in Boston and spread the word that the Americans actually had 1,800 barrels of powder! He even had large gunpowder barrels filled with sand placed in locations where British spies might see them. The tricks worked; the British held off attacking American lines long enough for new supplies of powder to be brought in from New York and Pennsylvania.

Tory spies were also well paid, and some surprising people turned out to be British moles. Take the case of Dr.

Paul Revere's "midnight ride" became the stuff of legend, thanks to a popular 19th-century poem.

THE SLAVE BECOMES A SPY

James Armistead was born a slave in 1748. With permission from his master, William Armistead, James joined the Continental Army in 1781, where he served under French commander the Marquis de Lafayette. Posing as a runaway slave who agreed to spy on the Americans, Armistead gained the trust of British General Charles Cornwallis and learned the general's strategy. Armistead's intelligence reports helped the Americans hatch a plan that kept the British from sending reinforcements to Cornwallis in Yorktown. As a result, Cornwallis was forced to surrender. James gained his freedom in 1787 with Lafayette's help. In gratitude, he changed his name to James Armistead Lafayette.

In 1781, the Marquis de Lafayette was only 24 years old as he led troops at the Siege of Yorktown.

Benjamin Church, a founding member of the Boston Sons of Liberty chapter and chief physician of the Continental Army. As far as the Patriot leaders were concerned, Church was one of their own. However, he was really a Tory, or Loyalist, who was being paid by Governor Gage to spy on the rebels. Some of his secret correspondence provided inside information about what the Americans were planning at Lexington and Concord and where their weapons were hidden. Church's treachery was finally discovered in October 1775, when he asked a female friend to deliver a letter written in code to a British officer. The woman was stopped by American sentries, who discovered the letter and brought it to General Washington's headquarters. Under questioning by the general himself, the woman revealed that Dr. Church was the letter writer. Washington had Church arrested and then asked codebreakers on his staff to decipher the message. They found it contained detailed information about American troop strength and supplies and even revealed plans for a future American attack on Canada. Church was given a quick trial and sentenced to prison and then banishment from the colonies. In 1777, he was placed on a ship sailing to the West Indies. He never arrived at his intended destination; the ship and Church's body were lost at sea.

Church was just one of many colonial political and military leaders who secretly supported the British or switched their allegiance during the war. The most infamous turncoat of all was American general and war hero Benedict Arnold. Angry at not receiving a promotion he thought he deserved and greedy for money to support a rich lifestyle, Arnold changed sides midway through the war. His *traitorous* actions were considered so terrible that people still sometimes call a person who betrays his country a "Benedict Arnold."

George Washington was both America's top general and its *spymaster*. He helped recruit American spies and often interrogated Tory spies such as Church. For example, after the British took control of the area around New York City in September 1776, Washington personally put out a request for a spy to go behind the British lines to report on troop size and movements. The man who volunteered,

Because British camps were in the midst of colonial towns, it became easy to spy on them.

21-year-old captain Nathan Hale, was brave but unlucky. After a week posing as a Dutch schoolteacher and gathering information, Hale was ready to return to the American side. He was caught by the British, however, who found secret notes hidden in his shoes. The next day, Hale was hanged as a spy. According to legend, Hale's last words were, "I only regret that I have but one life to lose for my country."

Later, Washington directed the formation of America's first spy network, the Culper Spy Ring, which operated around New York and uncovered information that was vital to the Continental Army's survival early in the war. Washington chose Benjamin Tallmadge, a classmate of Nathan Hale's at Yale College, to organize the group. Hale's death and heroism helped inspire the members of the new spy ring and made them more determined than ever to carry out covert, or undercover, actions to defeat the British.

The Culper Ring members, like most spies for both sides, were more often civilians than soldiers. Few people suspected that when shoemakers, farmers, shopkeepers, or housewives asked questions, they were probing for information. Workers could also move easily behind enemy lines in the guise of doing their jobs. Some of the best intelligence came from men and women who worked near enemy troops or *quartered* soldiers in their homes and listened in on their conversations. A number of women and girls proved to be especially valuable as spies and messengers because enemy soldiers tended to trust them or felt they were "too nice" for espionage.

There was another key reason that most spies were civilians. Spying was often looked on as dishonorable by those in the military. In fact, even before Nathan Hale volunteered, another officer had been asked and refused, saying, "I am willing to be shot [as a soldier in uniform] but not to dress in disguise and be hanged [as a spy]."

Unlike those civilians who worked for him in the Culper Ring, Tallmadge was an army officer.

CHAPTER TWO
COVERT ACTIONS *and* DIRTY TRICKS

SUN TZU, AN ANCIENT Chinese general and philosopher, once wrote, "All warfare is based on deception." By this he meant that, in order to win a war, a nation needs not only soldiers and weapons but also tricks and surprises to confuse enemies or steal their secrets. During the Revolutionary War, spies for both sides relied on deception, secrecy, and even some dirty tricks to help gain any advantage.

The members of the Culper Ring were especially good at deception. One trick involved using invisible ink. The ink they used was a special mixture known as "Jay's Sympathetic Stain," invented by colonial physician James Jay (who was the brother of Patriot leader John Jay). Ring members would use the stain to write secret messages between the lines of what appeared to be ordinary letters. As the ink dried, the messages would disappear. A reader had to brush the letter with a second chemical mixture to make the hidden words reappear. Despite the attempts at trickery, many of the spy messages were intercepted and deciphered.

The Culper Ring also devised an intricate system for carrying messages to Washington's staff. Spies would collect information behind enemy lines and write notes in code or invisible ink. Then they would

Instructions to wartime spies were conveyed through hidden handwritten messages or in person.

deliver the messages to a *courier* who would make a *dead drop* on the property of Abraham Woodhull, whose spy name was "Culper Senior." Woodhull would retrieve the notes and bring them to a small boat that would take them across Long Island Sound to Connecticut, where Tallmadge waited to convey them to wherever Washington was encamped. The boat's skipper could sail into any of six different coves. Woodhull learned which one by observing laundry hung on a clothesline by another Ring member, Anna Smith Strong. When a message was ready, Strong got a signal and would hang a black petticoat on her clothesline. Then she would hang several white handkerchiefs next to the petticoat. Four handkerchiefs meant "meet the boat at cove 4."

British spies also employed codes and dead drops for messages. For example, Edward Bancroft, a doctor from Connecticut, was living in France when the war broke out. Bancroft began as an American spy but agreed to become a double agent when the British offered him a salary of 500 pounds a year (equal to about $88,000 today). Bancroft attended many secret meetings between French and American leaders in Paris. When he learned vital information, he would write coded notes and place them inside a bottle with a string attached. Then he would hang the bottle inside a hollow tree in a Paris park. Someone from the British embassy, or government office,

would retrieve the bottle and replace it with another containing instructions for Bancroft. Once, when Bancroft was in London on an American mission, British agents protected his *cover* by arresting and imprisoning him. Then he was allowed to escape and return to France.

Another British spy trick was to cut messages into small pieces and transport

them inside small silver balls that spies could swallow if caught. That is

Edward Bancroft worked as a doctor in British Guiana (now Guyana) before moving to Europe.

what happened to Daniel Taylor, a British officer who agreed to cross American lines to deliver a message hidden in a silver ball. Taylor was captured, and the ball containing the message was discovered.

SHH! IT'S A SECRET

The Culper Spy Ring members were great at keeping secrets, but perhaps the biggest secrets of all were their true identities. Even George Washington knew them only by their code names or numbers. For example, the group's leader, known as Samuel Culper Sr., was actually Abraham Woodhull, a Long Island farmer. The code names helped protect the spies and their families from retaliation by the British. The names stayed secret until 1930, when historian Morton Pennypacker found letters and documents hidden in an old chest in an attic that uncovered the identities of all but one: 355.

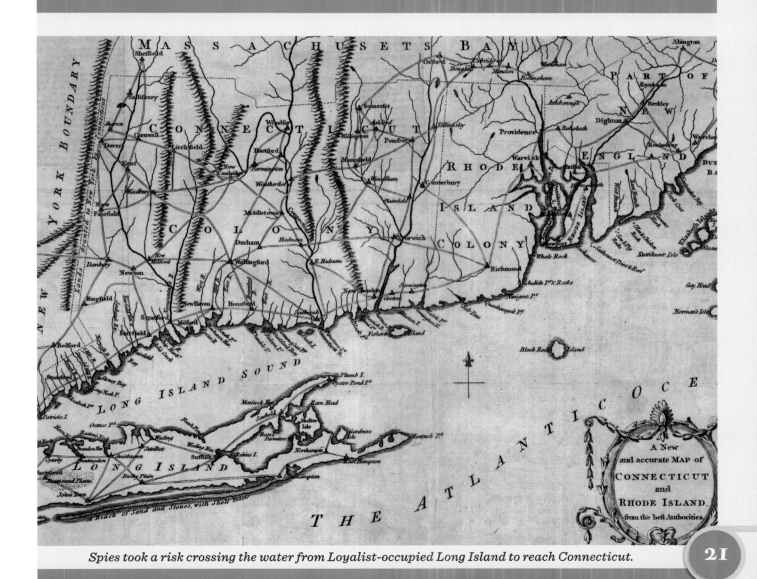

Spies took a risk crossing the water from Loyalist-occupied Long Island to reach Connecticut.

Taylor quickly swallowed the ball but was given medicine that caused him to vomit. The "recovered" evidence led to Taylor's execution.

Undercover spies were not the only ones practicing deception during the Revolutionary War. Even statesman Benjamin Franklin got into the act. Most people know that Franklin was an inventor, scientist, printer, and diplomat. But he was also a master at disinformation and propaganda, two important elements of espionage. Franklin spent the war years serving as America's representative in Paris. He hoped to convince French leaders to provide money, supplies, and troops to support the Americans against France's sworn enemy, Great Britain. The French were hesitant at first to side openly with the Americans—until Franklin found a sneaky way to speed up the process. He held private meetings with British representatives and hinted that the colonists might be willing to end their revolt and stay united with Britain. Then he met with French leaders and fooled them into thinking that the peace talks were more serious than they really were. Franklin even used Bancroft, whom he suspected was a British spy, to spread the disinformation. France signed a treaty of alliance in February 1778, agreeing to back the Americans, and French assistance helped turn the tide in the war. Franklin made sure that King George received a copy of the "secret" treaty within two days.

Later, Franklin carried out a successful propaganda campaign to decrease the morale of Hessian troops fighting with the British. He forged an outrageous letter from a German prince to the Hessian commander in America suggesting that severely wounded soldiers should be left to die. The "prince" claimed that Britain would pay Germany more for Hessians killed in battle. Franklin distributed copies of the letter in Great Britain and Germany and among Hessian regiments in America. The fake letter turned many Europeans against the war and led large numbers of Hessian troops to desert, or leave military service without waiting to be discharged.

Across the ocean in New York, a Polish-born Jew named Haym Salomon was also working to deceive Hessians and change their loyalties. Salomon was a successful broker in New York before the war

Franklin found favor with the court of Louis XVI and Marie-Antoinette and lived in France for nine years.

but was taken into custody after the British occupied the city. When British leaders learned that Salomon spoke excellent German, they hired him to translate for the Hessian commanders. What the British did not know was that Salomon was a member of the New York Sons of Liberty. He was the perfect mole. He reported what he learned from the Germans to American officers and also convinced many Hessians to change sides. When the British caught on, Salomon was arrested and sentenced to death. Luckily, he escaped and fled to Philadelphia, where he resumed selling bonds to help pay for the war. Besides raising money for the Patriot effort, Salomon gave much of his own wealth to help pay off American debts incurred during the war and fund fighting campaigns. In 1975, the U.S. Postal Service issued a stamp honoring Salomon as a "Financial Hero" of the Revolution.

American trickery throughout the war proved vital. A few of the most successful techniques included leaking false information about where the Patriot army might strike next, forging official-looking letters to encourage British generals to make poor military decisions, and planting moles such as Salomon and Enoch Crosby inside Tory groups to learn enemy secrets. All such measures proved to be keys to the eventual American victory.

In July 1779, a fleet of ships carrying French troops to aid the Americans arrived in Newport, Rhode Island. Knowing the French soldiers would be exhausted from their two-month transatlantic crossing, British forces began gathering for a deadly attack on Newport. Culper Ring members learned about the British plans and carried warning messages to both Washington's headquarters and the French commanders waiting on board in Newport. Washington then prepared "secret papers" detailing an imaginary plan to attack New York when the British army left for Rhode Island. These papers were allowed to fall into the hands of British spies, who delivered them to General Sir Henry Clinton, the British commander in chief. Clinton then ordered his soldiers to stay put in New York, giving the French troops time to leave their ships and prepare to join the fighting.

Among those who aided the Patriots' cause were families who lent their homes as wartime headquarters.

CHAPTER THREE
WOMEN MAKE *an* IMPACT

AMERICAN HISTORIAN CAROL BERKIN has written extensively about the special roles that women played before and during the Revolutionary War. She notes that women didn't make speeches, pass laws, toss tea into Boston Harbor, or sign declarations. Instead, their role had more to do with the practical economics of revolution. Colonial women led the boycott against buying British goods after passage of the Stamp and Tea acts. Many also refused to serve British tea in their homes or to sell British goods in the shops they ran.

Once the war began, women were often left to manage the everyday operations of farms and businesses. They also served as nurses, prepared and carried food to hungry soldiers, and knitted hats and scarves to keep the men warm. A number of fearless women and girls actually joined the war themselves, not as soldiers but as spies. They risked their lives crossing enemy lines to deliver secret messages or to uncover enemy secrets.

Women were so successful in their work as spies because many military leaders on both sides discounted their abilities to be sneaky and understand military matters well enough to write effective spy reports. The men were wrong. For example, in March 1777, a woman

Women spies could blend in with the battle scenes close to home as they cared for the fighters.

posing as a Tory farm owner walked right into the headquarters of British General William Howe to complain that American soldiers were stealing her grain. The woman, whose name has never been revealed, was a spy sent by Nathaniel Sackett, one of Washington's intelligence experts. While Howe listened to her complaints, the woman looked out his office windows and observed workers building flat-bottomed boats. Later, she casually conversed with the boat builders, who told her the boats would soon be used to carry British troops to Philadelphia. She reported the information to Sackett. Howe's forces did indeed capture Philadelphia a few months later. But by that time, Washington had set up a full spy network inside the city.

"Old Mom" Rinker was one member of that Philadelphia network. She would often sit knitting atop a rocky ledge near her family's tavern in the city. Sometimes she would "accidentally" let a ball of yarn in which she had hidden a secret message drop over the ledge. American soldiers on the lookout would retrieve the yarn and deliver it to their commander.

At least two women played key roles in the Culper Ring. One was Anna Smith Strong, whose coded clothesline was described earlier. The other's name remains a mystery; she is still referred to as "355." The Culper Ring often used numbers in its messages to stand for certain words, names, or places. For example, 711 was George Washington, 727 was New York, 745 was England, and 38 meant "attack." The number 355 stood for a woman whose identity was so secretive that it is still not known today. Historians have searched for information about 355. She is believed to have been part of a wealthy Tory family who had easy access to British leaders. She may have played an important role in uncovering Benedict Arnold's treason. She is also believed to have been eventually captured by the British and executed.

One female spy whose identity is known is Lydia Darragh from Philadelphia. Darragh's family were Quakers, members of a religious group that generally opposed

General William Howe gained command over all the British troops in America in September 1775.

THE SPY WHO NEVER WAS

In 1827, a Massachusetts printer named Luther Roby published a journal he claimed to have found. It was a first-person account of the supposedly real-life adventures of John Howe, a man who started out as a British spy during the Revolutionary War, then switched sides to join the Patriots, and later became a settler on the American frontier, among other escapades. The journal was packed with exciting tales, and Howe quickly became famous. The problem was that John Howe never existed; Roby had made him up. Roby fooled a lot of people for a long time. His hoax was not exposed until 1983!

A replica of the bridge in Concord over which the Minutemen drove back the redcoats stands today.

fighting and wars. That was one reason why British officers often met in the Darragh home to discuss war plans. The officers didn't know that Darragh's son was actually a soldier in Washington's army camped not far from Philadelphia. They also didn't know that Darragh herself would sometimes listen in on their meetings and report what she heard to American officers.

One night in December 1777, Darragh sneaked out of her bedroom and overheard a discussion about plans for a surprise attack on Washington's troops. Then she raced back to her room and locked the door. Before leaving the house, a British officer knocked on her door to make sure she was still securely inside. Darragh took some time to open the door and pretended to have just awoken from a deep sleep.

She knew she had to warn her son and the other American soldiers. Early the next morning, she took an empty flour sack and walked toward a mill just outside town. She easily obtained a pass to leave the city for her errand. She dropped the sack off at the mill and hurried toward an inn where she knew American spies sometimes met. On the way she ran into one of Washington's officers and gave him the news. When the British attacked, Washington's troops were ready and successfully turned them back.

A few days later, Darragh was brought in for questioning. The officer who had knocked on her door said he knew that *she* had been sleeping that night, but could anyone else have overheard the conversation in the parlor? Darragh replied truthfully, "No, everyone else was asleep."

One of the most unusual female spies was Patience Lovell Wright, a colonial artist famous for sculpting figures out of wax. In 1771, a fire in her New York studio melted many of her works. Her friend Jane Franklin suggested that she go to England where her brother Benjamin was serving as an ambassador from the colonies. Franklin introduced her to important people in London, who hired her to

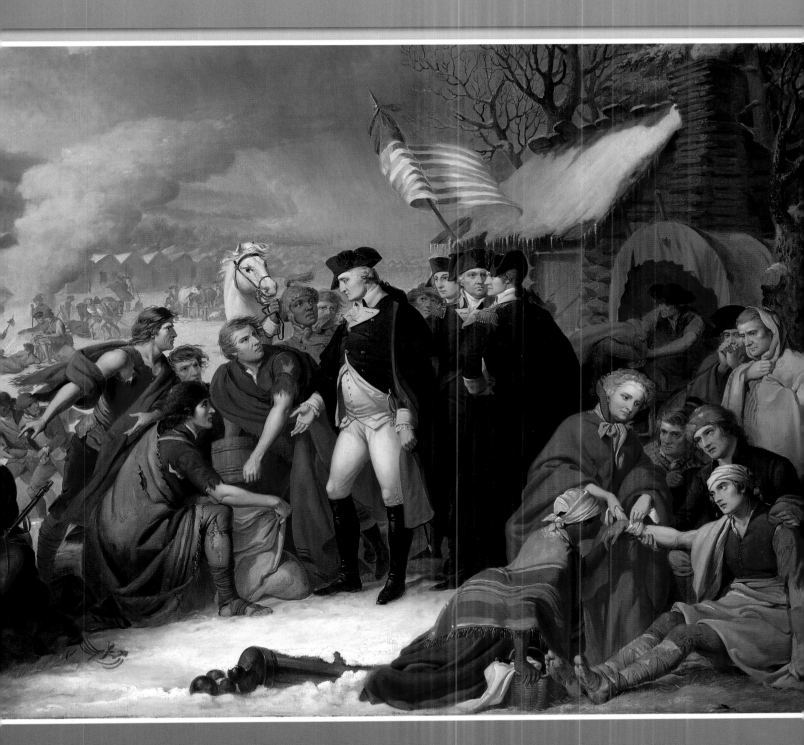

By the end of 1777, Washington's army badly needed rest as they wintered at Valley Forge.

sculpt their heads. She was still in London when the war broke out, and she often spoke out for American independence. That didn't stop British leaders from posing for her or speaking openly in front of her about war strategies. Wright wrote down what she learned. Then she hid secret messages inside some of the wax heads and sent them to her sister Rachel's gallery in Philadelphia. Her sister made sure the messages were delivered to Washington's staff members.

Even teenage girls such as Laodecea (sometimes spelled "Laodicia") "Dicey" Langston (15) and Emily Geiger (18), both from South Carolina, and Sybil Ludington (16) from Connecticut carried out vital spy missions for the Patriot cause during the war. Each of them was pressed into service to deliver warnings about impending British attacks on American troops. Ludington's daring horseback ride through the countryside in April 1777 has led some historians to call her "the female Paul Revere."

Not all colonial women supported the revolution, and a number of valuable female spies gathered intelligence for the British. Ann Bates was a Loyalist living near New York. Her husband worked as a cannon repairman for the British army and taught her a lot about weapons. She sometimes disguised herself as a peddler and sold goods inside American military camps. While there, she would count up the numbers of cannons and soldiers she observed and then report her findings to British officers. The information Bates supplied led to an important August 1778 Redcoat victory over American and French troops in Rhode Island.

A young French-speaking woman known as "Miss Jenny" served as a spy for one of the mercenary commanders fighting in America. She was tasked with finding ways to slip into the camps of French troops helping the Americans. Then she would report what she heard or observed to her German *handler*.

Sybil Ludington's ride is commemorated with an annual 31-mile (50 km) run in New York.

CHAPTER FOUR

FROM BETRAYAL *to* SUCCESS

BEING A SPY DURING the Revolutionary War required courage, quick thinking, deviousness, and luck. Not all spies were successful. Nathan Hale, for example, was caught and executed after only one week behind enemy lines. Some historians think that he was captured because he was too trusting. While scouting on Long Island, he struck up a conversation with a man named Robert Rogers, who hinted that he was secretly working for the Americans. It is possible that Hale said something that revealed his real loyalties, because soon afterward he was arrested. Since Hale was an army officer spying out of uniform, he was sentenced to hanging. (Had he been caught in uniform, he might have been given a military trial and imprisoned.)

General Washington was so upset when he learned Hale's fate that he made a key change in his espionage strategy. He decided to use only civilians to spy from then on. Washington turned to two trusted advisers to help him—Nathaniel Sackett and John Jay. Sackett was put in charge of spy recruitment and Jay in charge of counterespionage. Two of Sackett's most important recruits were the unnamed woman who reported the British plan to capture Philadelphia and a

Whereas Nathan Hale's life ended in 1776 (opposite), spymaster and lawyer John Jay (above) lived to age 83.

shoemaker from upstate New York named Enoch Crosby, who became America's first great spy hunter.

The events in Crosby's career would make for an exciting spy novel, and many experts believe that James Fenimore Cooper's 1821 novel *The Spy* was indeed based on Crosby's exploits. Crosby had two important qualities that made him an excellent spy hunter—he was resourceful, and he was friendly. In September 1776, he was riding toward New York to enlist in the Continental Army when he encountered a group of Tories. Crosby pretended to be a Tory as well, and the men spent hours talking about British war preparations. Late that night, Crosby slipped away and headed to Jay's headquarters nearby, where he reported what he had heard. Jay recognized Crosby's talent for espionage and persuaded him to become a spy hunter rather than a soldier. "Our greatest danger lies in our secret enemies," Jay told Crosby. "A man with your special abilities is [more valuable] than a regular soldier."

For the next two years, Crosby acted the part of a Tory cobbler. Several times he was captured, beaten, and imprisoned—always in the company of other Tories—yet he always "escaped" after passing along vital information he had learned. Crosby usually worked alone, but he did have help from other Patriots. One of his favorite helpers was Sybil Ludington, whose father was an American colonel.

They shared a code of secret signals, and the teen sometimes carried messages for Crosby.

Colonial cobblers repaired shoes but did not make them—that was the job of a cordwainer.

The spying activities of John Honeyman were detailed in a book written by one of his descendants in 1909. The book contained stories the family had shared for more than 125 years about a man who may have saved the American cause in December 1776 but never got credit for his actions. Were the stories based on factual events? Historians disagree. Because Honeyman did his spying undercover, there is very little evidence available to help prove or disprove the stories.

According to the tales, in late 1776, Washington's army had suffered several

MASKED MESSAGE

British General Sir Henry Clinton used a special technique to keep important messages from being read and understood by strangers or enemies. He would handwrite the message in a shape, such as an hourglass, in the middle of a page. Then he would add extra words to the left and right to fill out the lines on the page. The letter looked normal, but its true message was hidden. Clinton would then cut out the hourglass shape from a piece of stiff paper and send this "mask" separately. When the reader laid the mask atop the letter, the real message would be revealed.

Henry Clinton lived in New York as a teen but returned to America to fight the colonists in 1775.

key defeats in New Jersey and Pennsylvania. The troops were trapped on the Pennsylvania side of the Delaware River and hoped to cross the river to carry out a surprise attack on a Hessian camp near Trenton. Washington needed to pull a rabbit out of his hat of tricks. Months before, he had met with Honeyman, a farmer from New Jersey, and persuaded him to pretend that he was a Tory. Now the general had his men arrest his mole and throw him in jail. That night, a fire broke out in the jail area (possibly set at Washington's orders), and Honeyman escaped in a hail of gunfire from guards. He made his way to the Hessian camp, where he met with their commander. Honeyman told him that the American army was made up of inexperienced men who were tired of fighting and posed no threat in a battle. The reassured Hessian commander allowed his men to hold a holiday party, while Washington and his troops quietly crossed the Delaware. When the Americans attacked early the next morning, the Hessians were caught off guard and suffered devastating losses. The victory at Trenton set back the British cause and helped restore American confidence.

Over the next two years, Washington set up spy rings near both New York and Philadelphia. The Culper Ring members were particularly effective at uncovering British secrets and making the war more difficult for the Redcoats in New York and New England. Other spy groups were formed in southern colonies such as Georgia, South Carolina, and Virginia, where the British had gained control early in the war. Several times, these spies "allowed" forged documents to slip into the hands of British commanders. The documents tricked Redcoat leaders into believing that help was coming from other regiments. When reinforcements didn't arrive, the Americans scored several key victories.

Not every American espionage effort was a success, however. Perhaps the most upsetting failure involved Benedict Arnold's betrayal in March 1779. Arnold had been one of Washington's top

Emanuel Leutze's painting Washington Crossing the Delaware *(1851) is the iconic image of the event.*

officers, winning impressive victories in battles in upstate New York. Yet Arnold's flaws were his big ego and terrible temper. He was angry that he did not receive the recognition or financial rewards he felt he deserved. British spymaster Major John André targeted Arnold and offered him wealth and fame to change sides. For a promise of more than 10,000 pounds (worth upwards of $1.5 million today), Arnold began revealing American secrets to the British. He even offered to turn over to the enemy a key American fort he commanded at West Point, New York.

A series of unusual events helped end both Arnold's and André's spying careers. Before turning over West Point, Arnold demanded that André meet with him in person dressed in civilian clothes. There is some evidence that Culper Ring member 355 learned about this meeting and sent out an alert. While on his way back to the British lines, André encountered three American soldiers who were wearing British uniforms they had stolen to replace their own frayed clothing. Believing the men were British, André revealed his true identity. The men dragged him to American headquarters, where they discovered papers signed by Arnold hidden in his shoe. André was quickly sentenced to hang for spying while out of uniform. When British General Sir Henry Clinton learned about André's fate, he begged Washington to allow his trusted aide to be killed by firing squad as a gentleman instead of being hanged as a spy. Perhaps remembering the treatment of Nathan Hale, Washington refused.

When news of André's execution reached Arnold, he fled to New York City. He was given the rank of brigadier general in the British army and led British forces until war's end. In 1782, Arnold and his family moved to England. He returned briefly to North America for a stint in the merchant business and died nearly broke in London in 1801. He was never paid all the money he had been promised to betray his country.

The infamous date of September 21, 1780, went down in history as the day Arnold committed treason.

VICTORY *and* INDEPENDENCE

JUST AS ESPIONAGE ACTIVITY had preceded the fighting in 1775, it also pushed the war toward its conclusion in 1781. By April of that year, Redcoat troops in Southern states under General Charles Cornwallis were moving north toward Virginia, hoping to restore British control to George Washington's home colony. Meanwhile, General Sir Henry Clinton's troops were still occupying New York. The British were winning the war, but they were tired of fighting and upset that the conflict was costing so much.

Washington decided to gamble on a bold plan. The plan required good timing and excellent espionage. The first step was to join American troops near New York

With 17,000 troops to Cornwallis's 8,000, the colonists and French forced Britain to surrender.

with the French force based in New England. Step two was to move the combined forces to Virginia as quickly as possible while avoiding battles with Clinton's men up north. Step three was to find a way to keep Clinton from sending reinforcements to join Cornwallis.

Washington used his spy networks to convince Clinton that, while the Americans and French were indeed trying to unite, their real plan was to attack New York, not Virginia. To help deceive Clinton, an American double agent in New Jersey who was part of Clinton's spy team altered messages sent by other British spies. Clinton kept his army home as Washington's men and French forces were on the move. By the time Clinton realized what was happening, it was too late. Cornwallis's messages requesting reinforcements went unfulfilled. By late September, the American and French armies reached Virginia, where they were joined by a fleet of French warships. Cornwallis was trapped and forced to surrender at Yorktown. Defeated and exhausted from six years of war, the British decided to make peace and give up their claim to the American colonies. The Americans had won their independence.

COVERT OPS
THE CRIMINAL WHO SAVED A GENERAL

Isaac Ketcham was an unsuccessful criminal but a good snoop. In 1776, Ketcham joined a group planning to *counterfeit* the new paper money being printed to replace British pounds in America. He was caught and put in a New York jail. One day, Ketcham overheard several other inmates discussing plots to help the British defeat the Americans and capture New York. One plot involved kidnapping George Washington. Ketcham sent a note to his jailers saying he had very important information to trade for his freedom. A deal was made, and Ketcham told what he had learned. The plotters were soon caught, and Ketcham went free.

REVOLUTIONARY WAR

TIMELINE

FEBRUARY 10, 1763	The British, French, and Spanish sign the Treaty of Paris (1763), ending the French and Indian War.
MARCH 5, 1770	British soldiers fire into a crowd of Boston protesters, killing three. This becomes known as the "Boston Massacre."
DECEMBER 16, 1773	Members of the Sons of Liberty stage the Boston Tea Party.
OCTOBER 1774	Massachusetts colonists strengthen their militia and are expected to be ready to fight on a minute's notice, so they are called "Minutemen."
MARCH–APRIL 1775	British troops parade around Boston, and Massachusetts colonists adopt articles of war against the British.
APRIL 18–19, 1775	After British attempts to seize colonial weapons, the first battles of the American Revolution are fought at Lexington and Concord.
JUNE 15, 1775	George Washington is named commander in chief of American troops. He asks the Continental Congress to allocate funds for spying.
JULY 4, 1776	The Continental Congress adopts the Declaration of Independence. Soon afterward, the British score key victories and occupy New York City.
SEPTEMBER 22, 1776	Captain Nathan Hale, captured spying behind British lines in New York City, is executed.
DECEMBER 26, 1776	Disinformation spread by American spy John Honeyman helps Washington's troops surprise the Hessians near Trenton.

SEPTEMBER 26, 1777	British troops occupy Philadelphia. Washington has already set up a spy network inside the city.
FEBRUARY 6, 1778	French leaders, pressured by disinformation from Benjamin Franklin, sign the Treaty of Alliance with the Americans.
AUGUST 1778	Benjamin Tallmadge begins recruiting members for the Culper Spy Ring.
MAY 1779	British spymaster Major John André bribes Benedict Arnold to work for the British.
SEPTEMBER 21, 1780	André meets with Arnold. He is captured two days later and sentenced to be hanged as a spy.
AUGUST–OCTOBER 1781	American and French forces trap British General Cornwallis near Yorktown, Virginia. Cornwallis surrenders.
MARCH 1782	British prime minister Frederick North begins peace negotiations with the Americans.
APRIL 1783	More than 7,000 Loyalists set sail from New York to places in England, Europe, and Canada.
SEPTEMBER 3, 1783	The Treaty of Paris (1783) is signed, formally ending the American Revolution.
NOVEMBER 25, 1783	The last British troops leave New York City, on what is known as Evacuation Day.

GLOSSARY

COUNTERESPIONAGE—efforts made to prevent or block spying by an enemy

COUNTERFEIT—to make fake money that looks real in order to deceive or cheat others

COURIER—a messenger who delivers intelligence information

COVER—the made-up occupation or purpose of an agent

DEAD DROP—a secure location that usually includes a sealed container where spies and their handlers can exchange information or intelligence materials to avoid meeting in person

DECIPHER—to convert a coded message, or cipher, into normal text

DOUBLE AGENTS—spies who pretend to work for one country or organization while acting on behalf of another

HANDLER—a person who trains or is responsible for spies working in a certain place

INTELLIGENCE—information of political or military value uncovered and transmitted by a spy

MERCENARIES—professional soldiers who work for pay in a foreign country

MILITIAS—local armies composed of citizens rather than professional soldiers

MINUTEMEN—members of the Massachusetts militia who were expected to be ready for immediate military action

MOLE—an employee of one intelligence service who actually works for another service or who works undercover within the enemy group in order to gather intelligence

PATRIOT—a colonist who opposed British control in the Revolutionary War

PROPAGANDA—material distributed to promote a government's or group's point of view or to damage an opposing point of view; some propaganda is untrue or unfairly exaggerated

QUARTERED—lodged or stationed in a home, sometimes through force

SPY RINGS—groups of spies working together to carry out espionage

SPYMASTER—the person who recruits and is in charge of a group of spies

TORIES—American colonists who supported the side of the British in the Revolutionary War; also called Loyalists

TRAITOROUS—acting in a way that betrays one's country

SELECTED BIBLIOGRAPHY

Allen, Thomas B. *George Washington, Spymaster: How America Outspied the British and Won the Revolutionary War.* Washington, D.C.: National Geographic, 2004.

Bakeless, John. *Turncoats, Traitors, and Heroes: Espionage in the American Revolution.* New York: Da Capo, 1998.

Berkin, Carol. *Revolutionary Mothers: Women in the Struggle for America's Independence.* New York: Knopf, 2005.

Crowdy, Terry. *The Enemy Within: A History of Espionage.* Oxford: Osprey, 2006.

Janeczko, Paul B. *The Dark Game: True Spy Stories.* Somerville, Mass.: Candlewick Press, 2010.

Nagy, John A. *Invisible Ink: Spycraft of the American Revolution.* Yardley, Penn.: Westholme, 2010.

Raskin, Joseph and Edith Raskin. *Spies and Traitors: Tales of the Revolutionary and Civil Wars.* New York: Lothrop, Lee, and Shepard, 1976.

Rose, P. K. *The Founding Fathers of American Intelligence.* Washington, D.C.: Central Intelligence Agency, 1999. https://www.cia.gov/library /center-for-the-study-of-intelligence/csi-publications/books-and -monographs/the-founding-fathers-of-american-intelligence/art-1.html.

WEBSITES

NATIONAL WOMEN'S HISTORY MUSEUM SPIES EXHIBITION
http://www.nwhm.org/online-exhibits/spies/2.htm
Brief biographies of notable women spies and descriptions of their espionage activities from the American Revolution to the Cold War.

SPY LETTERS OF THE AMERICAN REVOLUTION
http://www.clements.umich.edu/exhibits/online/spies/index-main2.html
A comprehensive collection of letters, stories, and profiles of key military and espionage figures during the Revolutionary War.

NOTE: Every effort has been made to ensure that the websites listed above are suitable for children, that they have educational value, and that they contain no inappropriate material. However, because of the nature of the Internet, it is impossible to guarantee that these sites will remain active indefinitely or that their contents will not be altered.

INDEX